Silly Poems for Silly Kids

1) Silly Lily

Her name is Lily and she's so silly. She

would run in a square

and then just stay

there. She would

stair in the sky and

no one knew why

They think it's just

because her name

was Lily and she was

just silly

2) The Oscars

I was going to the

Oscars to see the

grand award and

when I got there I

was awfully bored so

I got up and started

to wiggle and the

whole crowd started

to giggle

3) Falling Jack

My name is Jack

And I just fell back

And when I fell

My head went whack

When it went whack

all

I saw was black

Now I'm okay and

it's a sunny day

4) When a dog barks

When a

dog

barks

what

could he

be

saying?
Could it

be that

he's

ready for

some

playing?

Or could

it be that

he wants

to go for

a walk?

Oh how

I wish

my dog

could

just talk

5) Mood for Food

I am in the mood for

food

But what kind sounds

good?

Do I want pizza or

ice cream?

Or to try to make a

sandwich I saw in a

dream

There are so many

things that I could try

and eat

For now I will think

as I sit in my seat

6) So many Animals

There are

so many

animals

that I want

A dog a cat

and a

bunny just

to start

Then

maybe a

pig and a

cow that

says moo,

but my

parents just

told me I'd

have to

clean up

the poo

Maybe less

animals

sound like

a plan

I know

what I want

now, a fish

named Stan

7) How do you feel?

Are you happy or are

you sad?

It's okay if you feel

mad

Feelings are

important

Feelings are real

Sometimes it's hard

to tell how you feel

You may use a color

of a picture on a

book, to tell a

grownup how you

feel just tell them to

look

I hope right now you

feel okay and that

you carry this feeling

to the rest of your

day

8) The Circus

I went to

the

circus

and it

wasn't

bad, but

the

clowns

smile

was

painted

wrong

and he

looked

sad

I wanted

to make

him

happy so

I tried to

dance

but no

matter

how

hard I

shook he

didn't

change

his look.

I hope

they

give him

a smile

tomorro

w maybe

I'll give

him

mine to

borrow

9) Bedtime

It's time to go to

sleep

It's time to go to bed

It's time to put our

jammies on

Then time to rest our

heads

Have a goodnight to

all little ones

I hope you enjoyed

this book and thought

it was fun

I hope your children enjoyed this book.

These are ones that I made up for my

son when he would start to cry as a

baby.